Rays Of Sunshine

Fahima Choudhury

GW00467836

BookLeaf
Publishing

Rays Of Sunshine © 2022 Fahima
Choudhury

All rights reserved.

No part of this publication may be
reproduced, stored in a retrieval system, or
transmitted, in any form or by any means,
electronic, mechanical, photocopying,
recording or otherwise, without the prior
written permission of the presenters.

Fahima Choudhury asserts the moral right
to be identified as author of this work.

Presentation by *BookLeaf Publishing*

Web: www.bookleafpub.com

E-mail: info@bookleafpub.com

ISBN: 9789395950381

First edition 2022

*This is dedicated to my Little Princess
Umaiza who loves my poetry. Also, to my
amazing Azeem and Naeem.
I love you lots and lots!*

*Thank you to my Ma and Dad for always
supporting me.*

*Thank you to my little ray of sunshine
Hannah for encouraging me to share my
poetry.*

*Thank you also to everyone supporting my
poetry page and reading this!*

My Little Princess Umaiza

In a world of fast transactions,
Where even personal gifts can be bought,
Sentiment delivered next-day to your door;
I want to show that you are to me, far more.

In a weak attempt to explain your worth,
I want to make something that make your eyes
sparkle,
I want to invest hours, not money, that society values,
They say "time is money," I disagree,
Time cannot be cheapened by economy.

Time is made of moments,
Memories of my smile radiating in your presence,
My eyes glow and my heart glistens;

Time is made of transitions,
Watching you grow,
From a baby caressed in my arms,
To twirling around me,
Skipping to and fro.

The very reason I wish to invest in you my time,
Is because you didn't pay me in money
For happiness.

You, my Princess,
Reminded me to value life,
When I forgot just what it was like…
To smile and mean it.

You didn't carry gifts,
You carried my heart so it felt lighter.
You didn't buy me warm clothes,
But your hugs thawed my heart.
You didn't hand me jewellery,
But you grabbed my hand up from boredom
And made me jump around with joy.

So thank you for bringing me the value of time,
And a happiness that is truly sublime.

Summer Days

I remember summer days filled with bliss,
Glowing crystals on my skin; a sun's kiss,
So clear in my mind, but feels like a dream,
I snap my eyes shut and let my smile beam.

First day on the beach, seeing the funfair,
The real memory were in the people there,
Now those sparkles evaporate to dust,
Gather on my brain like ant-coloured rust.

"Embrace change! Make experiences new!"
See new cannot be better without you,
"I miss the simpler times...", well that's a lie,
Life was never simple; we made time fly.

Now the days travel in a different form,
A race to the finish; avoid the storm,
Of rushing thoughts and a sadness that creeps,
A ghoul in the shadows whose grimace seeps.

So I daydream, for ignorance is bliss,
Evade the darkness and loved ones I miss,
But now and then, I remember those days,
And the smile falls back quickly on my face.

Flashbacks of light, radiating within,
From those summer days I'm enraptured in,
The true lesson I learned in all these days,
Is love remembers, it never decays.

Guarded

Unlatch the roof of the glass box,
Deposit your beating heart inside,
Let it circuit freely within,
Guarded in four walls to confide.

In time, it gasps for oxygen,
Running tired and depleted,
Blood seeping through the crevices,
Shedding red tears, defeated.

Fragile and anxious, it murmurs,
To survive, it craves connection,
Formulates a plot to break out,
From the deceit of protection.

Against edges, it thrashes and thumps,
And the once secure home does fracture,
Cracks fissure like in thin ice,
As the shards fire and rapture.

The veins it needed are obscured,
Shrivelled in absence of its source,
Like a wilted stem now deprived,
Both symbiotes live in remorse.

The glass box that was meant to shield,
Only made fragile what it concealed,
Pierced heart free but never cherished,
Left to rest in a body perished.

Blue Skies

As I stare in awe at the contoured sky,
Fading from turquoise to a range of blues,
The string of garden lights fade in and out,
In rhythm with blinking as my eyes snooze.

And my cheek rests gently on my hand,
As I gravitate towards the stars,
They twinkle and shimmer on and off,
Like headlights flashing on faulty cars.

Sitting at the same windowsill,
I watched fireworks and huddled,
Amazed by purple and gold sparks;
Shower the sky with lights muddled.

The swirls, swooshes and crashes,
Coloured lights dance way up high
The incandescent beauty,
Radiates within my eye.

Now I stare up and feel a slight cry,
How did so much change as time passed by?
And yet the same spot remains, white and cold,
I hope to sit there happy when I'm old.

Black Lives Matter

When did the aim become so sinister
You shoot at the civilians, call the prime
minister!
The president, a leader, some form of authority,
They look back at you with a shield of armour...

Funny how they think of defence when they attack,
Funny how they run for humans but empathy they
lack,
It's crazy how they can shoot 7 times in the back,
Why did you shoot them?
No reason, we just know he's **black**.

Was it marijuana, "the war on drugs?"
Who are you kidding? You don't value lives,
You belt out excuses to justify the crimes.

When it's all said and done,
Drugs can cause harm, addiction,
But you pull that trigger like a grenade,
Murder; the real drug bringing you satisfaction.

Deprive them of money but still want taxes,
Make them homeless but you send them faxes,
And when you post those videos of them shouting,
You try to make it out like "they asked for it".

But Floyd had a minor counterfeit,
And Sandra Bland was a proud activist,
And Tamir Rice was just a boy playing outside,
And Arbery was running so
WHERE ON EARTH CAN THEY HIDE?

Don't make excuses, it's the whole institution,
From slavery, you took advantage of
The 13th Amendment.
You made black people a profiting scheme,
Took their labour and hard work to make the seams
For that American flag you label as *freedom*,
Stitched red with their blood and blue
With the jumpsuits you dress them.

Maybe the many stars are for
How many eyes are facing up,
While you take her mugshot and claim
She did it to herself.

Wander the World's Wonders

Do you look at the world's wonders,
And dream one day to wander?
Vision blurs to scorching heat waves,
The pyramids of Giza stand under.

Tread over the dusty hands,
Of past dynasties that built,
Thousands of miles from earth,
The Great Wall upholds guilt.

Discover the gushing water,
Soft mountains of sandstone,
Inhabited by an Arabian tribe,
Petra does not beg to be known.

Admire the mountain that looms over,
Watch mossy land handshake the sea,
The beauty of Rio de Janeiro,
Lights up crowded houses of agony.

Get lost in the varying heights,
Steps form an intricate maze,
Dive in clouds of Machu Picchu,
Above woven bright green that amaze.

Watch the clouds enshroud,
Chichen Itza in shade,
Sunlight splitting the projection,
Of a serpent slither the cascade.

Hear the battles cry,
The roar of bears enraged,
Echo around the Colosseum,
Leaving evil entertained.

Glistening on the river,
The marble of Taj Mahal shimmers,
Parchinkari of stones and calligraphy,
Art of the Mughal empire glimmers.

Make sure your heart explores,
From depths of the sea to mountains tall,
Dream from a bird's eye view and soar,
For inspiration will always enthral.

Seasons

Autumn leaves burning bright,
Mirror the blazing rays of light,
Crisp to touch as they disintegrate,
Delicate in your hands, they wait.

Leaves crawl into the lakes,
Where the brisk cold invades,
Sheets of ice that duvet,
Joyful waters that freely waved.

Single snowflakes slap the window,
And blend to an army of snow below.
Crunches under your rubber boots,
Snowmen made with twigs and roots.

The icy mists runs yet lingers,
Striking the winds, your nose and fingers,
As the sun twirls around again,
To grow herbs, spices and cayenne.

Beautiful buds begin to bloom,
Baking juicy fruit pies, taste the fume.
Daffodils, tulips, sunflowers,
Burst with a radiance that showers.

Smiles diffuse across the land,
A spring in your step on grassland,
As new life begins to pop and peek,
Ready for summer and looking chic!

The rays return, shimmering white,
Beaches glisten, sands fly in excite,
Taste the ice lollies and lemonade,
Bathe under the umbrella shade.

Life is in seasons, each one unique,
With glee, sadness, emotions that leak.
Each has purpose, timestamps on life,
Spend each quarter, in riches or strife?

Her

A shutter of darkness falls from the sky,
Sparkling jewels scattered high,
Twinkling in frightened eyes below,
As she tiptoes in the freezing meadow.

The grass crunches under her sole,
As the fear within grasps her soul,
Sharply turning around, she feels a glare,
Eyes of darkness hollowed and stare.

She quickens her pace, watching her breath,
Invade the air like the smell of death,
An awful foreshadow of what could be,
If she didn't escape hurriedly.

Losing signal on her phone,
Searches for light on her own,
In front of her is a dark maze,
An unclear view in the dreary haze.

Through the path she tiptoes,
Camera flashes in the shadows,
Keys tightened, balled in her fist,
As she whispers through the mist.

So unpredictable is the danger,
Yet all too common, the harm,
Can a woman walk safely?
Will she ever feel calm?

Ember Lies

Everything the ember touches is
Demolished by flames.
Glowing in the sky like fireflies.
Orange stars flickering,
Under the moonlight.

Suddenly the light fades.
The sinister ashes hurtle down.

Like mini comets,
Like a thousand newsletter pieces,
Burning across the canvas of stars.

A flame that once provided,
Glow, wonder and warmth,
Now creates panic, destruction.
A grey sombre remorse.

Book of Thoughts

If only, if only,
The book nearly cried,
They'd turn just a page,
And a little bit more.

They'd see more than a story,
Or a little anecdote,
They could learn a life lesson,
Or recall a lasting quote.

If you gave me just a pinch of your time,
A gentle patience and curious mind,
Your complex ideas could merge with mine,
Convoluted to the brim, you may find.

I could transport you to another world,
To the vast galaxies or smallest cell,
Through the sandy beaches or grainy moon,
Are woven mysteries I crave to tell.

All inside from the depths of my mind,
Lodged in my skull with nowhere to go,
Yet I can make you picture crown jewels,
Or dusty mines they belonged to so.

Don't you see, I connect to your senses,
Visualise a sea of many places,
Or smell the sweet fumes of chocolate vapours,
And taste vanilla frosting off cases.

Listen to the pitter patter of rain,
Feel silky banisters glaze your fingers,
Do realise I am more than I seem,
I leave you with a feeling that lingers.

I can remind of your bravery,
The cute wrinkle bouncing in your smile,
So don't tell me words aren't powerful,
When this nurtured after a while.

So let your ideas blossom,
For I was once lovingly taught,
A lasting quote from spoken words,
A pen has more might than a sword.

A Moment

I am an old song fading on a dusty river,
From a creaking, rusty car,
On sandy, coastal roads.

I am a lonely star strung in the sky,
Sparkling in swift moments,
In a web of galaxies.

I am the dust gathering on the bookshelf,
Near a caramel, coffee ring,
And a cotton filled chair.

I am the sharp wind in the cold breeze,
Rushing past your rosy smile,
On a bright, sunny dawn.

I am simply a moment,
An encounter in your fulfilling life,
Hoping to be a significant memory.

Lost at Sea

A boat emerges on shore,
The waves whisper to push more,
Smash the sands with ambition,
The vessel lay flat, in station.

Sails that once wrestled the wind,
Tussled dark storms in a death grip,
Now hang, like a defeated flag,
In surrender to a life on land.

Oh the joys of wild adventure,
Fiery horizons brushed left to right,
The seagulls would sing under the sun,
As you now navigate the end run.

To finally settle and find peace here,
Where home and love were once near.
You find a golden locket woven in grain,
"I will love you for always, beyond the pain."

No longer in water, yet lost at sea,
Buried in the sands of time is she,
Ponder the day you left her behind,
Would you now have changed your mind?

Jungle

Sprinting through the twigs entwined,
Wind sharp like needles in your face,
Bewildered eyes lost in time,
Frantic; searching for safe space.

You dart through the crisp branches,
And fear grapples your mind tight,
Heart racing in tune with feet,
Paralysed inside with fright.

Wander further in the jungle,
Sinister vines crawl to escape,
Sunlight shimmers through scattered leaves,
And through woven twigs, creatures scrape.

You wade through countless branches,
Echoes whistle through the air,
Rip in ear drums like tissue,
As you turn quickly and glare.

Nature enlightens your vision,
Eyes absorbed in emerald green,
Invade your cells intricately,
Like details on stitched lace unseen.

More noises and wildlife appear,
Eery snakes slithering around,

Locked onto you as a target,
As they plot and writhe on the ground.

You stand there frozen in time,
Try taking everything in,
Breath interrupted by gasps,
Easing the struggles within.

So you carry on,
Stepping left and right,
Persistence is the key,
Not paralysed by fright.
And you wander alone,
With just you; flesh and bone,
One with nature; inhale oxygen,
Walk the earth in adoration.

The sun makes you smile,
Absorbed in your skin,
You look up to the sky,
To search from within.

Through all of the darkness,
At last, a beam of light,
You creep through the last trees,
The sparkling lake in sight.

You can sit down now, breathe,
Let your body unwind,
Amazing how tangled you feel,
In the depths of your mind.

Magnifying Glass

Focus on me like lenses.
Resolution in your image clear,
See me distinctly in your point of view,
Until glass shatters like your perspective.
The blurry deceit of your false ideas appear.
Cracks remain, a broken vision of expectations.
High pedestal placed, what you idealised of me.
Busy moulding a concept...just accept me truly!
No longer objectively fair, search every minute
detail of what you like and dislike. Tired eyes.
When pointing one finger, three return to you.
The only question that, like death, remains,
Can a shattered relationship repair?
If you magnify a subject and
fixate a heat spot, anger.
You need to take
Precaution.
Watch out.
Careful.
Or you
might
start
a fire.
Over.
You
and
Me.

Insomnia

The common question is..
Are you a morning bird or night owl?
If identified as the latter,
You're met with a scowl.

But if the early bird catches the worm,
Surely by night, they drift into a whirl,
Of dizzy thoughts in the still night.
Only movement of stars and leaves,
Sparkling and rustling in sight.

While the early bird rejuvenates,
The night owl is sharp,
Refined as marble, energy like a spark.
Maybe by day, they are drowsy, unsettled,
Overwhelmed by tasks, daily battles.

The stillness of the night unveils their plan,
And the night owl's precision
Like the target of a marksman.
These precious hours, they grasp with talons,
To organise their vision and balance.

Speaking of vision, gain perspective,
For an early bird or night owl keeps focused,
Both are driven, as they lift their wings,
Neither are better, based on these musings.

They can both be welcomed,
As their rhythms intertwine,
So the morning be productive,
And the night also shine.

Quarantine

Running and racing,
Sweating and pacing,
Vines wind up to the sky,
Thorns sharp, idly stand by.

Trying to escape out the twisted maze,
Patterns like maps, eyes lost and glazed,
Look left and right but not a way out,
It all looks the same, no clue about.

I feel the sweat grasping my neck,
Am I in danger, will I make it back?
Pressing my head like an off button,
To stop the whizzing thoughts.

Wait a second, I'm not outside,
I fear the maze sprouting inside,
With nerves entangled and spreading,
Latching onto darkness like venom.

The real danger lurks within,
A monster so hateful, it's hidden,
In the depths of your mind,
The most twisted tunnel you'll find.

You ask me why I find it hard to close my eyes,
I'm not really sure, low iron? She sighs.
Tired of knowing she's fighting a battle,
With no armour, no shield, but she visits often.

So at night when the stars are glistening,
She feels the grasp on her blanket tightening,
She closes her eyes, the warning display signs,
'Enter at your own risk', eyes ready to cry.

So will you enter unarmed or carry a light?
No need to fear, you gleam within so bright.
The brain may appear a tangled mess,
But look deeper within, you'll see a fortress.
A community of neurons connected together,
To bring you grey, white and all kinds of matter.

In darkness, you'll be terrified,
How do I make my way out?
But through light, you'll see,
There's a clear pattern, don't doubt.

School Memories

I still remember my first day at school,
Woke up early, dressed, tried to look cool,
My sister dropped me off late and I was fuming,
But they thought she was my mum
And my smile was blooming.

She stuttered in embarrassment so I said "bye!"
Signed in, rushed to the hall as we waited by,
We were assigned forms and how nerve wracking!
A classroom of newbies to crack on with.

Boy! Were we loud for a bunch of girls,
A force to be reckoned with delicate curls,
A bundle of personalities mixed in a room,
So different and wild, buds fighting to bloom.

We had food fights and screaming matches,
And wow, did we sing!
And let's face it, there were tears,
Sometimes it was stifling.

We still came together and had so many laughs,
We grew as a team and made memories to last,
Competing in sport, performing drama and dance,
Laughing at teachers, getting kicked out of class.

We improved on ourselves,
We came back together.
Now that quote finally makes sense,
On a painting seen from the first day,
While I was sitting tense.

The journey of a thousand miles
Begins with a single step,
We did it and
I'm excited to see what is next.

Palestine

From the rivers to the sea,
Palestine will be free.
Israel teach to invade,
Evil should not receive aid.

They laugh and smile,
At children suffering,
And beat the civilians,
With cameras not stopping.

The skies polluted with bombs,
The air with skunk water,
The land in rubble,
Blood of a daughter.

Or mother or father or little baby,
From Haifa to Gaza to Sheikh Jarrah,
I shake and tremble with tears,
As I watch through screens for years.

These beautiful children smile,
At the smallest of joys,
Hearts so pure but eyes glazed,
From shock and trauma.

We live in a world,
Where we need to convince,
With statistics and laws,
When millions are displaced and killed.

Imagine how destructive the media can be,
To make you believe that,
A 3.8 billion funded defence are defenceless,
And that limbs can be dangerous.

I pray I see a day,
In Gardens of Paradise,
Where rivers flow beneath the innocent
Palestinians' feet and they feel eternal peace.
Ameen.
No more red rivers to carry their corpses away.

From the rivers to the sea,
Palestine will be free.

Ingram Content Group UK Ltd.
Milton Keynes UK
UKHW021957060423
419712UK00013B/1570

9 789395 950381